Children's Authors

Kate DiCamillo

Jill C. Wheeler

ABDO Publishing Company

visit us at
www.abdopublishing.com

Published by ABDO Publishing Company, 8000 West 78th Street, Edina, Minnesota 55439.
Copyright © 2009 by Abdo Consulting Group, Inc. International copyrights reserved in all
countries. No part of this book may be reproduced in any form without written permission from the
publisher. The Checkerboard Library™ is a trademark and logo of ABDO Publishing Company.

Printed in the United States of America, North Mankato, Minnesota.
012009
102011
Cover Photo: Brett Patterson / brettphoto.com
Interior Photos: AP Images pp. 10, 17, 18; Brett Patterson / brettphoto.com pp. 5, 9, 21; Corbis
    p. 13; Getty Images p. 15; iStockphoto p. 7

Editors: Tamara L. Britton, Megan M. Gunderson
Art Direction: Neil Klinepier

Library of Congress Cataloging-in-Publication Data

Wheeler, Jill C., 1964-
  Kate DiCamillo / Jill C. Wheeler.
     p. cm. -- (Children's authors)
  Includes bibliographical references and index.
   ISBN 978-1-60453-076-6
   1. DiCamillo, Kate--Juvenile literature. 2. Authors, American--21st century--Biography--Juvenile
literature. I. Title.

  PS3604.I23Z95 2009
  813'.6--dc22
   [B]
                                  2008004801

Contents

Master Storyteller

Kate DiCamillo is the author of the award-winning books *Because of Winn-Dixie* and *The Tale of Despereaux: Being the Story of a Mouse, a Princess, Some Soup, and a Spool of Thread*. Much of what DiCamillo writes is inspired by her childhood experiences. When she was young, DiCamillo did not like it when adults talked to her as if she could not understand. Today, she refuses to do that to her readers.

DiCamillo also works to present life realistically in her books. She knows that the real world can be scary and **complicated**. That is why her characters often deal with frightening and complicated topics, too.

It took DiCamillo many years to succeed. She received nearly 500 rejection letters before a publisher accepted her first book! Since then, more than 7 million copies of DiCamillo's books have sold worldwide. Her work has been translated into 25 languages.

Kate DiCamillo

A Sickly Child

Kate DiCamillo was born on March 25, 1964, in Philadelphia, Pennsylvania. Her father, Adolph Louis, was an **orthodontist**. Her mother, Betty Lee, was a teacher. Kate has an older brother named Curt.

As a child, Kate was often sick. She suffered from childhood diseases such as measles and chicken pox. In addition, Kate had **pneumonia** every winter for the first five years of her life!

Doctors advised Kate's parents to consider moving to a warmer climate. They thought living someplace warm would improve Kate's health. So when Kate was five years old, her family moved to Florida.

Kate liked Florida. But, the move did not keep her from getting sick. She still missed a lot of school. Kate spent most of her time inside by herself instead of outside playing with friends.

Kate thinks her childhood illnesses helped her become a writer. Because she was alone so much, she discovered how to entertain herself with her own imagination. Kate also learned how to observe others very closely. For example, she learned to be on the lookout for the next **thermometer** or tongue **depressor**!

Florida has a warm climate and snowfall is a rare event. The average winter temperature is 72 degrees Fahrenheit (22°C)!

Dogs, Friends, and Books

When Kate was six years old, her parents separated. Kate, her mother, and her brother settled in Clermont, Florida. Kate thinks the separation may have influenced her writing. Many of her characters have single-parent families.

Kate made the best of the situation. She had a beloved black standard poodle named Nanette. For fun, Kate dressed Nanette in clothes!

Kate met her first best friend, Trinky, when a boy at their nursery school stole Kate's blocks. Trinky quickly told the teacher about the boy's bad behavior. Kate was thrilled that someone had stood up for her.

When not playing with dogs and friends, Kate found friends in books and stories. She has fond memories of listening to her father tell made-up fairy tales. And, her mother often read to her.

Later in school, Kate read everything she could get her hands on. Her favorite childhood books included *The Secret*

Garden by Frances Hodgson Burnett, *The Twenty-One Balloons* by William Pène du Bois, and *Ribsy* by Beverly Cleary.

Kate remembers being spooked after reading *Black Beauty* by Anna Sewell. For years afterward, she refused to read a book with an animal on its cover. Kate did not read *Charlotte's Web* by E.B. White for that reason. She was afraid something bad would happen to the pig pictured on the cover!

Kate jokes that she never would have read some of her own books. Many have an animal on the cover!

Training to Be a Writer

After graduating from high school, Kate attended several colleges. In 1987, she earned an English **degree** from the University of Florida in Gainesville, Florida.

It was during college that Kate first thought about becoming a writer. Several professors commented on her writing abilities.

One experience in particular stands out in Kate's mind. For a writing class, Kate's first assignment was an essay. The essay had to be 500 words long. Kate delayed writing it until the day before it was due. That night, she saw a street musician outside a grocery store.

In her essay, Kate described the musician. She handed it in the next day. A week later, she was pleased when the teacher singled out her essay in class. He said it was a good example of truly paying attention to something and then recording it.

Still, Kate was disappointed. The teacher had not said the essay was a fine piece of writing. However, years later she realized that the teacher had pointed out something very important. Today, Kate's work is often recognized for its fine attention to detail.

Opposite page: *The University of Florida is one of the nation's most renowned research universities. Researchers there invented the sports drink Gatorade!*

Climate Change

DiCamillo knew after she graduated from college that she wanted to be a writer. Yet, it was a long time before she started to write. In the meantime, DiCamillo had many jobs. She worked at a campground and in a greenhouse. She also worked at Walt Disney World in Orlando, Florida.

In 1994, DiCamillo decided to make a big change. One of her friends was moving to Minneapolis, Minnesota. DiCamillo decided to go, too.

In Minneapolis, DiCamillo worked for a book **distributor**. She filled orders for children's books. As she worked, DiCamillo read some of the books. She was impressed with the quality of children's literature. DiCamillo decided to try writing for children.

DiCamillo began her first children's book during one of Minnesota's long, cold winters. She missed Florida's warm weather. She missed having a dog, too. Dogs had always been important to DiCamillo. However, her apartment did not allow them.

One night as she was falling asleep, DiCamillo heard a voice in her head. It said, "I have a dog named Winn-Dixie." DiCamillo did not know where the voice had come from. Yet she chose to pay attention.

DiCamillo began getting up at 5 AM to write before work. She wrote about a little girl named India Opal Buloni and her dog, Winn-Dixie.

Minneapolis has a cold climate and can get more than 45 inches (114 cm) of snow each year. The average winter temperature is 15 degrees Fahrenheit (-9°C)!

A Book at Last

DiCamillo wanted an **editor** to take a look at her **manuscript**. One day at work, DiCamillo met a salesperson from Candlewick Press. She asked the salesperson for help. The woman agreed to give the manuscript to an editor.

Unfortunately, that editor soon left Candlewick. DiCamillo's manuscript was packed into a box. It lay undiscovered until 1998. Finally, a young editor found it and read it. The editor knew right away that it was a book worth publishing.

That same year, DiCamillo had applied for and received a **grant**. The grant program gave money to writers so they could pay their bills while focusing on their writing.

For the next two years, DiCamillo worked with the editor to get the manuscript just right. It was finally published in 2000. *Because of Winn-Dixie* became a *New York Times* best seller. The following year, it was named a **Newbery Honor Book**.

A movie based on Because of Winn-Dixie was released in 2005. AnnaSophia Robb played India Opal. Three Picardy Shepherds played Winn-Dixie.

Newbery Winner

The **Newbery Honor** for *Because of Winn-Dixie* was a remarkable achievement. But, it also made DiCamillo a little nervous. She felt that she had to write another great book right away or people would not like her anymore. Soon, the right story began to unfold.

Like *Because of Winn-Dixie*, this story was about a child and an animal in the South. This time, the main characters were a boy named Rob and a caged tiger. *The Tiger Rising* was published in 2001. It was a **National Book Award** finalist.

DiCamillo's third book began with a comment from a young boy. She had gone to Florida to visit her best friend. There, her friend's eight-year-old son asked for a favor.

The boy asked DiCamillo to write a story about "an unlikely hero with extremely large ears." The request took DiCamillo by surprise. She told him that she did not write books on command.

Yet his words kept running around in her mind. Before long, DiCamillo was writing about a hero with very large ears.

The hero was a mouse named Despereaux Tilling. His adventures became *The Tale of Despereaux: Being the Story of a Mouse, a Princess, Some Soup, and a Spool of Thread*. The book was published in 2003. The following year, it won the **Newbery Medal**.

DiCamillo remembers receiving the 7 AM phone call telling her of the award. She was so excited she asked the caller to repeat the news three times!

Cynthia Richey holds a copy of The Tale of Despereaux as she awards it the Newbery Medal.

Rabbits, Pigs, and Picture Books

DiCamillo was thrilled with winning the **Newbery Medal**. But the following year was just as exciting. In 2005, DiCamillo introduced her readers to a new character.

Mercy Watson is a pig, and a spoiled one at that! She loves buttered toast and getting into trouble. Candlewick Press published *Mercy Watson to the Rescue* in 2005.

Since then, DiCamillo has written other Mercy Watson books. *Mercy Watson Goes for a Ride* was a 2007 **Theodor Seuss Geisel Honor Book**.

Meanwhile, DiCamillo was hard at work on another book. A friend had given her a gift of a rabbit doll. For some reason, she had a vision of the rabbit underwater.

DiCamillo began writing a picture book about it. Yet the story just kept going on and on. DiCamillo's vision turned into a novel. *The Miraculous Journey of Edward Tulane* was published in 2006. It won the **Boston Globe-Horn Book Award** for fiction.

In October 2007, DiCamillo published her first picture book. *Great Joy* is the story of a helpful young girl, an organ grinder, and his monkey. Bagram Ibatoulline illustrated *Great Joy*. It became a *New York Times* best seller.

Opposite page: *In 2008, an animated movie of* **The Tale of Despereaux** *was released.*

Sparking Stories

Today, DiCamillo is busier than ever! In addition to her own writing, she teaches writing classes at Hamline University in Saint Paul, Minnesota. She also accepts many speaking engagements.

DiCamillo still challenges herself to write two pages a day, five days a week. This schedule is very effective! Her fifth Mercy Watson book, *Mercy Watson Thinks Like a Pig*, was published in July 2008. And *Louise, The Adventures of a Chicken* was released that September.

Kate DiCamillo has no plans to slow down. In fact, she carries a notebook with her. In it she keeps a list of ideas for future writing projects. She calls her ideas "sparks." Fortunately for her fans, it is a pretty long list!

Opposite page: *DiCamillo enjoys stretching the vocabulary of young readers. Her books contain unusual words such as perfidy and porcine.*

Glossary

Boston Globe-Horn Book Award - an award the *Boston Globe* and Horn Book Inc. give to the year's best picture, fiction, and nonfiction books.

complicated - having elaborately interconnected parts.

degree - a title given by a college to its graduates after they have completed their studies.

depressor - a device for pressing something down or to one side.

distribute - to give out or deliver something. A person or a company that distributes goods is called a distributor.

editor - a person who is in charge of preparing a work for publication.

grant - a gift of money to be used for a special purpose.

manuscript - a book or an article written by hand or typed before being published.

National Book Award - an award given annually by the National Book Foundation to books written by American citizens and published in the United States in the categories of fiction, nonfiction, poetry, and young people's literature.

Newbery Medal - an award given by the American Library Association to the author of the year's best children's book. Runners-up are called Newbery Honor Books.

orthodontist - a dentist whose specialty is straightening teeth.

pneumonia (nu-MOH-nyuh) - a disease that affects the lungs and may cause fever, coughing, or difficulty breathing.

Theodor Seuss Geisel Award - an award given by the American Library Association to the author and illustrator of the year's most distinguished American English-language book for beginning readers published in the United States. Runners up are called Theodor Seuss Geisel Honor Books.

thermometer - a device for measuring temperature.

Web Sites

To learn more about Kate DiCamillo, visit ABDO Publishing Company on the World Wide Web at **www.abdopublishing.com**. Web sites about Kate DiCamillo are featured on our Book Links page. These links are routinely monitored and updated to provide the most current information available.

Index